Holy Land

Holy Land

POEMS

ANGELA ALAIMO O'DONNELL

IRON
PEN

PARACLETE PRESS
BREWSTER, MASSACHUSETTS

For My Whole and Holy Family,
Especially Our Lou

2022 First Printing

Holy Land: Poems

Copyright © 2022 by Angela Alaimo O'Donnell

ISBN 978-1-64060-784-2

The Iron Pen name and logo are trademarks of Paraclete Press.

Library of Congress Cataloging-in-Publication Data
Names: O'Donnell, Angela Alaimo, author.
Title: Holy land : poems / Angela Alaimo O'Donnell.
Description: Brewster, Massachusetts : Iron Pen/Paraclete Press, 2022. |
    Summary: "These poems honor both the holiness and the wholeness of our
    world-while honoring the holiness and wholeness of our broken
    humanity"-- Provided by publisher.
Identifiers: LCCN 2022018975 (print) | LCCN 2022018976 (ebook) | ISBN
    9781640607842 (trade paperback) | ISBN 9781640607859 (epub) | ISBN
    9781640607866 (pdf)
Subjects: BISAC: POETRY / Subjects & Themes / Inspirational & Religious |
    POETRY / Subjects & Themes / Places | LCGFT: Poetry.
Classification: LCC PS3615.D653 H65 2022 (print) | LCC PS3615.D653
    (ebook) | DDC 811/.6--dc23/eng/20220420
LC record available at https://lccn.loc.gov/2022018975
LC ebook record available at https://lccn.loc.gov/2022018976

10 9 8 7 6 5 4 3 2 1

Cover design: Paraclete Design
Cover image: Vincent Van Gogh, The Sower, 1888. Wikimedia Commons

Published by Paraclete Press
Brewster, Massachusetts
www.paracletepress.com

Printed in the United States of America

"Remove your sandals from your feet, for the place on
which you are standing is holy ground."
—Exodus 3:5

———————

"The Holy Land is everywhere."
—Black Elk

CONTENTS

III Ancestral Lands

IV Sounding the Days

V Literary Islands

VI. Border Songs
A Mercy of Triolets

EPILOGUE

The Journey

We were warned about the weather
but we made the journey anyway.
We hoped for something better
than the lost lives others led.
We were in love and we were wed
to the future, brighter days
than any we'd seen in our bleak town.
Call it hope. Each new place we found
was rich in what our old world lacked.
We heard new music we learned to play.
Once you leave you can't go back
to the dead city blues you'd known
as a child. We braved wild wind, hard rain.
And when the weather was bad, we sang.

I

Christ Sightings

"For Christ plays in ten thousand places."

—GERARD MANLEY HOPKINS, "As Kingfishers Catch Fire"

The Storm Chaser

The Mount of Beatitudes
October 16, 2019
7 AM

Running along the Sea of Galilee,
I see you in your boat, tall brown
man that you are, standing in the prow,
arms raised in supplication to the skies,
wind-whipped tunic blowing wild & high
as the waves that have paralyzed your friends,
who have hit the deck and now lie prone
on the sodden wood, dumb as stone
and waiting for what surely is the end,
so low in the boat I can't even see them.
You alone are all might, pure motion
in the shape of a god, this small ocean
no match for your infinite love—for them,
for the sky, for the sea. And, yes, even for me.

The Thief

*"Jesus . . . turned around in the crowd and said
'Who touched my garments?'" —Mark 5:31
Encounter Chapel, Magdala*

When she touched him she stole his fire,
woman Prometheus who wouldn't take
No for an answer. She was bold
and full of blood, despised creature
who crept along the edges of
the swollen crowd, when she spied gold,
bore her broken body to the sun
center of the Lord's pulsing love.
Call it a miracle it took two to make.
Call it a Reverse Midas Moment.
But tell it true and tell it blunt.
Her sudden bout of faith. Her long torment.
Her taking what her old god would not give.
Long after his dying she would live.

The Mount of Olives

"And the Scribes & Pharisees brought unto him
a woman taken in adultery."
—John 8:3

I know this much. She didn't speak.
Women are never believed when they do.
She stood up to be judged. Didn't seek
mercy from those men. She knew
they'd kill her, do what they wanted to do
or not. Depending on one man
they wanted to snare in their net
webbed and woven of half-true lies.
Deciding who lives and who dies
blood sport to them, but not Him.
He bent down and wrote in the sand
their names and beside them each one's sins,
each daily failing, each man's debt.
One by one the sinners left.

Ichthys at the Jordan

The West Bank, Palestine

We waded into those easy waters
like children in search of a blessing.
Tiny fish flashed and gathered,
nipped our feet, a strange welcoming.
It was as if they'd been waiting
for us, knew we had been following
from sea to sea to see the Fisher King.
While we waded we wondered
if they greeted you, too,
as John poured the Jordan on your
bare head. That moment you were sure
who you were, was the sky this blue,
the sun this warm, the water this sweet,
fish gathering and flashing at your feet?

Lazarus

Bethany, Palestine

Deep beneath the street we found you.
The passage narrow, the stairway steep.
A space barely big enough to
stand in, let alone lie. The rock
walls thick, the ceiling low. We ducked
and still hit our heads. Tiny Lazarus.
Your story bigger than you and us.
Four feet tall, ten feet under-
ground. I could not help but wonder
how you heard your name, the women weep,
life come knocking at death's cold door,
you fast trapped and fast asleep.
Christ's call so loud, such a surprise,
what could you do but wake and rise?

A Song for Gethsemane

A rose blooms in Gethsemane
in the grass where you wept.

Far from their home in Galilee
your fisher friends slept.

High above the olive trees
the moon floated her love.

The whole garden grieved
with you, nightingale & dove.

The child your mother once conceived
and raised in Nazareth

brought to weep & brought to bleed,
endure a lonely death.

Here amid the garden's gloom
your blood and tears still bloom.

Via Dolorosa

"Station Five, Chapel of St. Simon of Cyrene:
To the right of the lintel in the corner of the wall at shoulder height is a
smooth stone with a hollow where Jesus supposedly placed his hand when
he stumbled while carrying the cross."
—The Skeptic's Guide to The Holy Land

Put your hand in my side, Christ said
to Thomas. I put my hand in
the hole in the wall. It was just
the size of a suffering man's,
it was just the size of my sin.
I faltered, too. I did not trust
the stone or flesh. Both men are dead.
But in this place I felt our hands
touch. The space was just the span
of my five fingers. Nothing can
convince me now he was not there,
that Magdalene's unruly hair
was not soothed by that healing hand,
that he was not more than a man.

Ghazel at the Western Wall

Jerusalem

The women at the Western Wall
rock their bodies as they pray.

The women at the Western Wall
hold their children as they sway

back and forth before the Western Wall.
The child on your hip will pray

if you take her to the Western Wall.
A small girl will watch and play

a woman's role at the Western Wall.
She will become one day

a mother at the Western Wall
whose child learns how to pray

by rocking at the Western Wall,
remembering the way

her mother at the Western Wall
taught her how to pray.

Magdalene's Mistake

*"They have taken away my lord . . .
and I don't know where they have put him."*
—John 20:13

She knew these things: a body doesn't walk.
Soldiers can't be trusted. Gossips will talk.

She made her way there in the early dark.
She knew the stories—Noah and the Ark,

Jonah and the whale, David and the stone,
the things a man can accomplish alone.

Even so, she couldn't quite conceive
how a dead god could just up and leave

his beloveds behind, stricken with grief.
The empty days and nights, however brief,

reminding them of what they'd left behind—
death without rising for all of their kind.

She watched day dawn. Saw the budged rock.
Wept for all the bodies that would never walk.

The Women

"And the angel said to them, 'Do not be afraid! I know that you are seeking Jesus the crucified. He is not here, for he has been raised just as he said. Come and see the place where he lay.'"
—Matthew 28:3–4

Because the angel spoke lightning, white and hot
Because the guards lay stunned like living stones
Because the rock that blocked the cave was budged
Because their arms held pots of oil and dry spice
Because he shone so bright he hurt their eyes
Because they'd been weeping instead of sleeping
Because it was dawn and the first birds were up
Because they'd slipped out of the house in the dark
Because the children would be waking soon
Because their breasts were full of morning milk
Because their hearts leapt like new lambs
Because he was their Lord and was not dead
Because the air was chilly, their robes thin,
They ran from the tomb praising him.

The Land of Resurrection

"Just as Jonah was in the belly of the whale
3 days and 3 nights
So will the Son of Man be in the heart of the earth
3 days and 3 nights."
—*The Gospel According to St. Matthew*

You have to enter darkness in order
to learn light. Immerse yourself in earth
before you can climb out. Inhabit flesh
so that you can be birthed. Endure disorder
before you can know peace. It is worth
the effort, the chance to see afresh
the old world you are sick of looking at.
The sun rising in its daily way,
the tired sky, its shades of blue & gray,
the green hills, the desert hot & flat.
All of it surprise to newly risen
eyes, correction to your whale belly vision.
The world won't change, but human beings can.
3 days & 3 nights made Christ a new man.

The Son God

Easter Sunday
Fells Point, Baltimore

Easter morning and Christ rises,
walks across the harbor to the sea
blessing the birds, the glistening fishes,
speaks the only beauty that can be
spoken by a dead man who has risen,
hid within the earth, a tattered sail
far beyond mending, yet was given
a mast and a spar, a brisk tail-
wind to ride his way to glory,
to navigate the channels and the lanes,
waving to the boats that set out early,
all the while he sings the same refrain,
the Son God's unearthly water song
as the birds and the fish sing along.

Easter Monday

Christ comes, a knock on the door when I least
expect him. Espresso in hand I pop open
the screen door that sticks in every kind
of weather. *Peace be with you*, he breathes
as he brushes by, sniffing for toast,
an egg, some fish. We eat our breakfast
in the too-small nook, our four knees
touching beneath the table. We find
little to discuss, though lots has happened
over the last two thousand years,
disaster since he last appeared
become our daily bread. His lined
face says he knows what we don't say.
I ask him if this time he plans to stay.

The Ninety-Ninth Name of God

More lonely than I really want to be
I find your name written on the back of
my hand where I used to write the names of
boys that I loved and wanted near me,
the letters thick & slick with Sharpie ink
scrawled and awkward on my thin hand skin.
Of all the girls in class you wouldn't think
I'd be the one to like boys so much and sin,
to be full of want for their attention,
but I was. It wasn't due to a lack
of love at home. I had sisters, a million
cousins, a Mom I loved who loved me back.
Even then it was you that I craved,
your name on my hand, in my heart engraved.

Advent

Village of Bronxville, New York

Because Christ walks the earth in late
December, peering into houses lit
from within, lifting the lids off stew pots,
tasting the salt and the light with equal
zeal, arriving just in time for the meal,
bread in his left hand, blessing in his right,
drinking wine, hoping to spend the night
in a place where he is greeted and received
a guest,
          I leave the back door unlocked,
lift the black latch on the garden gate,
wander the lanes of our little town
trying my luck, knowing that just around
the bend walks God, empty and full of need,
hunger only soup and love can feed.

Christ Sighting: December 25th

Church of the Nativity, Bethlehem

Here comes the dark, the dearth of the year.
And here comes Christ again. Born when he's least
expected and most needed. Now and here
in the midst of famine comes this feast
fit for fools surrounded by the ruin
we have made of our own earth, the rivers
black with mourning for the jewels they once were,
the air thick with smoke from the charred trees.
Now in the darkness we fall to our knees
in wonder at the baby birthed just for us.
We deserve nothing. No small sign of luck.
In a world ripped by rage, choked with anger,
love lies sleeping in a dirty manger.

II

Crossing Ireland

"Out there . . .
  In the old man-killing parishes
  I will feel lost,
  Unhappy and at home."

—SEAMUS HEANEY, "The Tollund Man"

On Not Belonging in Ireland

Our Aer Lingus flies through Irish skies,
and I know I'm not at home
well before my feet touch the Tarmac.

Filing into Shannon, we take our places
in the long line of Irish ex-pats
whose cousins left as hopeful as they arrive.

Here I am clear extra, exotic
by Irish measure, if not New York's,
my dark hair and olive hands a sign.

You don't look Catholic, says the ex-priest
who left Queens and his cassock behind
for this spot at Hughes' bar, *An Spidéil.*

Italian—or Jew—what's the difference?
says the glint in his Irish eye.
Nothing of you begins here, where we do—

his American accent stronger than mine,
me with my traitorous poet's ear
who loves all music better than my own.

At two weeks' end, I'll speak with a lilt,
the song of the Island sown in my dreams,
my foreign heart more native than she seems.

County Kerry

In the shadow of MacGillycuddy Reeks

Unreal, the way we walk among them
full of our bangers and eggs,
clad in our smart mackintoshes
and good boots, safe from the rain
that pierces them like bullets from a dark god.

There is death out here in the beauty.
A hunger remembered in the earth.
The mountain rises slant, like mercy.
The slow slope of light eases the grace
under all the suffering and sorrow,
beyond the dark-ringed eyes of the haunted
whose hunger can know no end.

We call it *drama, romance, history*.
We trespass on their mystery.

Tigh Mholly

An Spidéil

Yer makin' the Yanks' Tour, are ye?
Peadar said, Cian smiling behind the bar
pouring 4 pints for his new American friends,

our 100-mile drive from Kerry to here
amusing to a man for whom the next
county is another country away.

He told us the history of the pub,
the clock that stopped at Mholly's daughter's birth
a century gone, ticked past the time

while he walked us from stone room to stone room
naming the faces in the Stations on the walls,
a Celtic Virgil leading a mis-guided tour.

All the while we drank the famous Guinness
drawn from Mholly's lines laid long ago
making it the best on the Spidéil Road,

while we argued poetry, Barack O'Bama,
the slant of the light on Connemara cliffs,
no new thing fine as the old.

What he knew he knew sure as his own hand
and wouldn't take *no* for an answer:
Heaney was a hack, Donegal men dishonest,

and Clifden as far as you'll need to go
should you need to leave home for awhile
and you know you'll be needing to come back.

On Pilgrimage

Glendalough Monastery

They're great ones for travel, the Irish Saints,
or so the map announces with its names
of mountains, towns, and old holy wells.

Brigid loved Liscannor's Hag's Head grandeur—
and the ground gushed in sympathy, healed all harm
long after she left to tend the fires of Kildare.

Patrick climbed the Croagh above Clew Bay
and hove a great bell past the edge
ringing in the era of snake-less Eire,

while Brendan rowed his Bantry boat from coast
to coast, baptizing pagans and blessing babies,
before setting out, at last, for America

like so many of his kin and kind
in centuries to come. How rare the saint
who homes, the blackbird's brood hatching in his hand.

Hopkins in Ireland

This is no country for young men
the fire in whose bones could set aflame
the fields of peat and bogs of cured bodies
that lie beneath the turf of grinning green.

The damp gathers everywhere,
in corners, joints, and hearts,
weighting all that leaps to dance and beats to time
and wetting wood and hay and kindling sticks.

To this land you brought the blaze of God's love
and glowing coals you took from every tongue
to make it catch and light up all the world.

Who couldn't guess the smoke and snuff and smolder
of all that burned within Christ's poet's soul
by the fog and chill, the everlasting rain?

And yet you flamed most bright and brief
in the heart of the desolate dark,
fire against the ashen sky
the color of spent embers.

Carrowmore

"The cairn-heaped grassy hill
Where passionate Maeve is stony-still."
—W. B. Yeats

Circled by mountains, the land lies silent,
the stone-strewn fields of County Sligo,
and if you didn't know you wouldn't know
the scattered heaps of granite rocks are tombs.

Passage tombs, they're called, though there's no way
out, only a doorway into darkness
we've been passing through for seven thousand years
since ancient feet first walked these fields.

No Celtic cross redeems the lost ones,
its telltale wheel of life at death's crux,
only stones on stones, still air beneath
the turtle back that holds each dolmen down.

All flesh is ash, the old ones discovered,
as they gave their bodies to the fire,
men and women refined to bone and shell
and mingled in the conjugal cairn.

Small comfort in the face of the mystery
not having to endure it alone,
the circle of stones around each mound
walling off the knowers and the known.

Stone heaps shadow Knocknarea,
bide in silence, visited by dumb sheep,
rough riddles to the eyes of passing strangers
wherein our unremembered selves forever sleep.

Inis Mór Tour

Tomás, the crazy man of Árann,
waved his worn map at me,
his red minibus idling patiently.

I'll take ye on tour in yer very own van,
the 80-Euro fee, he promised, a steal.
We were charmed, fooled, dumbed into the deal.

Great stout fellows! he bellowed at the seals
who wallowed on the island's western shore
as if they'd heard and answered him before.

He told the same 3 jokes: *seven t'ousand stone
walls on the island, though I don't know
who counted 'em!* he'd intone,

then laugh the mirthless laugh of the mad
while we all stared straight ahead
hoping he'd keep the van on the road

wracked with glee at the touring Yanks who
came so far to see mere rocks
and paid 80 Euro to do so

(that being the 4th joke—the one he would think
and not tell, savor it in his thoughts
as he'd wave to his neighbors with a sly wink).

We made his day. And he made ours, if truth
be told about an islandful of lies.
There's no romance in being marooned,

no great honor or special dignity
living life at the mercy of the merciless sea.
The truth not on his tongue was in his eyes—
the profit in what fools prize.

Dun Aengus

You prefer the edge, I the hold.
That day at Dun Aengus, on cliffs
above the boulder-smashing sea,
you set your boot in crack and craw
leaning out beyond the ending
of the ground I loved to feel be-
neath my feet. Great granite towers
seemed to sway through clouds and rain,
no pick or rock to keep you
from the three-hundred-foot free fall.

Nowhere near the edge, I lost my grip.
Words I flung the wind hurled
back, while you clicked and held
the world I couldn't look upon.
At last I turned away,
stepped east to tame my giddy pulse,
and set my feet towards the imaginary keep.

Now you love to show the photographs
of that fierce place, claimed and unsubdued.
Some of me appears in a picture,
my back set against the iron sky,
my wild heart a match for the sea.

Fir/Mna

Here in the corner of the world-as-was
the old words still speak true. The Skellig Ring
around the rose of Kerry's coast drops us
down mountains to Gaeltacht shore. The waves sing
the same song on the newer coast we know
but in strange language and a minor key.
The same things happen, but they happen slow.
The names for us different as *you* from *me*.

Here I am *mna* to your *fir*,
small swells in a surge of Irish thrust
as if a syllable were enough
to circumscribe our being here.
You face the wind and call to me,
my name as foreign as that sea.

On Leaving *Éire*

She is all blue, air & earth, sea & sky.
She is bog, the color of ruin.
She is a long song across the water.

I don't belong.
I could make my self a life there.

III

Ancestral Lands

"By the rivers of Babylon, there we sat down,
yea, we wept, when we remembered Zion."

—Psalm 137:1

"Where you come from is gone, where
you thought you were going to was
never there, and where you are is no
good unless you can get away from it."

—Flannery O'Connor, *Wise Blood*

Immigrant Song

Pittston, Pennsylvania

There you go wearing your dirty heart
on your sleeve again, your mining men
and breaker boys' faces smudged with coal,
lunch buckets open, sandwiches sooty
with the prints of their blackened hands,
telling the story of their sorry
days, years spent in darkness while the sun
tried to shine through thick clouds that part
only rarely, so unlike bright Sicily,
its sapphire seas and fields of gold,
Etna's rich volcanic sands,
fishing boats skirting the vivid land
rife with life and color, all you lack,
how much they would give and give to go back.

The Land of Childhood

Hickory Run, The Pocono Mountains

We would rise early to pack the picnic,
dump the ice in the red metal cooler,
stack the bowls of cold food our mom had fixed—
potato salad, coleslaw, fried chicken—
pull the baked ziti hot from the oven,
bag sweet sausages wrapped in butcher paper
from Sperazza's store. We were Italians
and loved July 4th like Americans.
The Pontiac loaded with lunch and children,
my father would drive the back country roads
to the distant mountains, the spring-fed lake
where we'd swim all day till our arms & legs ached,
till our lips turned blue from the biting cold.
The day would never end. We would never be old.

304 Washington Street

West Wyoming, Pennsylvania

Squat and square, her pea-green shingles
made her strange on our straight street
lined by wood white houses,
their faces bland and neat.

We'd raise the window sashes.
We'd open the screen doors.
We'd stage our family drama.
They always wanted more—

the neighbors who disdained us,
who knew we didn't fit
inside their wood white world,
who didn't give a shit

when one of us was dying,
when all of us grew poor,
absorbed in their not-watching.
We don't live there anymore.

Praise Song for My Older Siblings

for Gregory, Rose Ann & Charlene

The way you struck out ahead of us
and swam rough waters with confidence
that we could barely muster. The luster
of our loves and deeds shone never
so bright as yours. You were all do
and drama, your reds redder, your blues
deep as any sky or wine dark sea.
Beside you we felt small and paltry,
unable to catch up, a lifetime
of falling further and further behind.
Yet you were always kind—
tossed us lifelines though you'd had none.
To you we'd be forever young,
the lucky daughter, the beloved son.

The Land of Last Things

Indian River Hospice Center
February 1, 2010

Ten years ago I packed a bag,
put on my blackest dress and caught a cab
which took me to a plane with my name
on the manifest. That day it rained
all the way from New York to Palm Beach.
My brother, who was not dead yet, picked me
up and drove me fast, trying to reach
you, mother, before you passed. I heard each
minute tick by, watched the door closing shut
as night fell on us like a hammer. I cut
you out of my heart long ago, and there
I was, rushing to put you back. I cared
for nothing but this—to arrive at your side,
to claim you with this kiss before you died.

Tell Me

St. Mary's Cemetery,
Wilkes-Barre, Pennsylvania

Tell me something beautiful, my mother.
Sing me a song from your house beneath the ground.
Tell me the story of the kidnapped daughter
filched from the sunlit world and dragged down,

down to dark rooms with ceilings of stone
where walls, carved from ice, can hold no fire,
where beauty is a rumor of memory,
loneliness the ghost of dead desire.

Tell me how she chews the iron chains,
slides the bracelets off her wounded feet,
straddles the boulders of Hell's ravine,
breeches the surface, dirty but neat,

free from the god who dogged her so long.
Tell me that story. Sing me that song.

The Land of Daughterhood

April 25, 2021
53rd Anniversary of My Father's Death

So long ago you left us. You're gone
now longer than you were here. A man
forever absent in my mind. I barely
knew you, despite my 8 years as your
daughter. You were distant, a rarely
happy father, with too many children
and not enough love or money.
This our story. Death a ticket out
of the mess you made with our mother,
us being the mess. I thought
all men disliked their kids, but then
I learned that we were different, not
like the families we watched on TV,
those flickering shadows we ached to be.

The Land of Resilience

Knoxville Medical Center
For Lou

My brother is in the hospital, again.
Struck by a stroke three days ago,
he slowly recovers his speech, his mind,
the flex of his arms & legs. He can
sip from a straw & swallow like a champ.
He doesn't know what day it is, but knows
how to beat like a heart, how to flow
blood through his narrowed veins. The same
body that ran fast, absorbed the shock
of blocks on a football field & didn't stop
running does what it was made to do. Time
doesn't change who we are. He's still the man
who life has hammered, who meets his rough end
in a wrecked car, in a brawling bar

                     and gets back up again.

The Land of Long Marriage

For Charlene & Richard

Finding a space in the green day to tell
a story, just one story. The one about
my sister who keeps her husband alive
with three shots of insulin a day. His gout
and unhealed heel wounds make it hell
to walk or sit or even to survive
as he must—if not then why the fuss,
the three good meals she makes, the silly jokes
she tells to take his mind off the pain? Thus
they live, man and wife, as if this life
were worth the courage. They walk the knife
edge of the grief that's coming. This is no hoax,
no dress rehearsal. This is all they get,
making the most of what isn't over yet.

The Land of Extravagance

*"I fear chiefly lest my expression may not be extravagant enough,
may not wander far enough beyond the narrow limits
of my daily experience,
so as to be adequate to the truth."*
—*Henry David Thoreau,* Walden

"Enough! or Too much!"
—*William Blake,* The Marriage of Heaven & Hell

The line between enough and too much
runs thin as isinglass, fast as fire,
excess as easy to the touch
as surfeit where there is desire.
A glass of wine accrues to two,
a taste of meat becomes a meal,
the night I thought I'd spend with you
lasts forty years. It is the seal
that fates me, the deal that breaks me,
this inburnt inability
to reckon time for what it's worth,
my 60 years upon this earth
not near enough for those my kind
to learn how not to cross that line.

Two Mornings
The Land of Now & Then

New York & North Carolina

Against this morning's silence I write
something into being, something true.

A laughing baby, his mother's pure delight.
This yellow morning sitting here with you.

The smell of coffee, the promise of toast.
The sleepy baby, milk-drunk & nodding.

His father lifts him with the utmost
care, lays him gently on the bedding.

Meanwhile we count the cats, the winter birds
that pass through our yard unsuspecting

that they are being watched, put into words.
The child is in his crib, softly breathing.

We live alone and happy, you & me,
as we were those mornings that used to be.

The Land of Birth

St. Joseph's Hospital
Baltimore, Maryland

Another dazzling October 6th
like the one you were born on, Baby
Boy. Wild blue sky, wind in the trees,
Fall falling all around us, while we
watched from our birth bed, warm & dry,
newly used to one another's breath,
weary from our labor and happy
as only the exhausted can be
who have just made life out of nothing.
That moment the sweetest kind of high
I'd ever known or have known since.
The mad branches tossed & nodding.
Time stopped still and about to start.
Your heft against my smitten heart.

Consecration

St. Matthew's Church
Baltimore, Maryland

I woke to baby shoes. Buster Browns
with tan stitching and stiff black soles.
The hard sound they made slapping against
the concrete floor of the basement church.
My child running up and down the aisles
howling his hooligan's howl. My mother's urge
to chase him, make him stop. The tense
wait for the host to be brought down
to the dish, back to earth from the high
holy place it had been lifted so we
could see, undistracted, unconfused
by the noise of our hearts as they beat,
the sirens in the street, the bad news
from a passing car, those baby shoes.

The Land of Dreams

"Not in entire forgetfulness,
And not in utter nakedness,
But trailing clouds of glory do we come
From God, who is our home."
—William Wordsworth, "Intimations of Immortality"

Last night I dreamed of a baby boy.
He wrung his small hands and spoke adult words.
Everything's a blessing & all is holy,
lisped the vatic infant under the sink.
He made us laugh, brought us to the brink
of wonder. We knew it was absurd.
(And what was he doing under the sink?)
But, still, he spoke to us, and, still, we knew
that this child who didn't have a clue
about suffering was telling the truth,
that somehow, despite his extreme youth,
he had glimpsed the vision mystics do,
wrapped in his blanket of baby blue,
and delivered himself to me and you.

Love's Song

Tempe, Arizona
10/10/2020
for Patrick & Nacho

You are the rose of my heart, he said,
channeling Johnny Cash, both being men who
always speak truth & always wear black.
Once words are spoken, they can't be taken back.
She knew he was in it for love. So two
singular souls found themselves matched & mated
and knew they were meant to be wed.
They wasted no time. Love that is fated
is love that won't wait. A wild rose is red,
the color of passion. Red, the color of art.
Red the common color of these two red hearts
that beat today together, synced in song forever.

You are the rose of my heart, he said in one breath.
You are the love of my life, she said, *till undeath*.

The Wave

New York
11/11/2017
for Will & Laura

She waved to him from the balcony
as if it pained her to see him go.
Hair pulled back, white dress on, she stood
serene above the chaos of Queens,
the grind and dust of roaring engines,
a mother pushing a stroller, her
burqa billowing behind her
in the hot breeze, a delivery boy
pedaling his stripped-down bike.

In the car beside me, my son waved back.
Though he'd be gone for hours, he would
return. A fact both lovers had to know.
Still. All day long I could not forget
the wave, his Romeo to her Juliet.

A Cana Blessing

Minneapolis, Minnesota
6/29/2013
for Charles & Elise

When Christ came to Cana he changed the game.
There could not be a wedding without wine.
The water that he stirred could not remain the same.
The wine as it aged would get better with time.

And so Christ comes to touch these lovers here,
to change young love into love full & fine,
love that pours out plenty from year to year.
love in such excess it is theirs and yours and mine.

This is their miracle. Now love comes to call
and knocks on every heart in this room
as these lovers pledge nothing less than all
for this day through the dawn of doom.

Let us bear witness, raise our glasses up,
to so much love spilling out the cup.

The House

Bronxville, New York

At night I set my house on fire.
   By day I build it up again.
The night's a cheat. The night's a liar.
   The day's my confidante and friend.
The flames consume the things I bought
   and brought to fill an empty space.
Things I loved and things I thought
   could love me back. I made this place
a storehouse of our old desires.
   Now nothing else will do but fire
to purge the past from our full rooms,
   to leave what doesn't serve in ruins,
to sweep away the dust and ash,
   to make a new house that won't last.

Home Bound

Baltimore, Maryland

The city where I don't belong
tempts me with its promises of
home, sings to me the same old song
of water, sunful skies, and love,
all I left behind and can't get back.
Still, my heart beats to the tune.
My life here a fiction and a fact,
ghosts glimpsed amid the sweet ruins,
stones I hoard and palm, things of earth,
that feel, for all the world, like beauty,
objects of inestimable worth
that ballast me, keep me steady,
right me when I know I'm going wrong
in the city I live now and don't belong.

IV

Sounding the Days

"Time is but the stream I go a-fishing in. I drink at it; but while I drink I see the sandy bottom and detect how shallow it is. Its thin current slides away, but eternity remains."

—HENRY DAVID THOREAU, *Walden*

Terre et Lune

Cape Hatteras,
North Carolina

Ah, la lune est brisée, said the child
to the half moon. She stared, pointing her finger
at the night sky. Her sudden true and wild
thought broke over us both, like the waves
the moon pulled from the fevered sea.
We stood beneath the stars we couldn't see
but knew were there in pairs, while the single
moon shone its broken light. There are days
when the world seems ruined beyond repair,
a doomed ship whose crew has lived recklessly.
We wave our white flags but can't be saved.
We flash our SOS to no one there
except the moon, earth's companionable ghost,
the world's blessed and broken communion host.

The Land of Luminaries

Kitty Hawk,
North Carolina

This morning I stood between the sun
and moon. They spoke to one
another, throwing light and catching it,
like friends who know each other's minds.
I listened with my eyes and saw their song.
It was full of love and full of deep long-
ing. The dance they did kept the two apart.
They looked upon one another's face
knowing that they never would embrace.
All the while they kept our planet lit,
earth the child of their collective heart,
we inheritors of their art,
the catch and throw of light, the world awake,
as I stood between them watching day break.

Late Light in August

Here we are again at the end of things.
The cricket strikes up his late summer surge.
The empty robin's nest no longer sings.
The heat of the day and cool nights converge
bringing us to the insistence of now.
We never know why, we never know how
we arrive at the same place every year.
The end of one thing brings all ends nearer.
        So let's light the candles, uncork the wine.
        Let's dine by starlight, set out the fine
        silver that shines in the slivered moon,
        touch each pointed knife, each curving spoon,
        eat our small feast at the table of love,
        make it a night we'll later dream of.

Bodies in Motion

August 12, 2020

Last night we waited for meteors,
streaks of fire to flame across the sky,
to light up our darkness, take us by surprise,
remind us of the fact that time flies
and so do we, though we seem to be still,
glued to earth as it wheels and tilts
its way around our solid sun,
which is no more solid than the air
we move through, the unseen ether
that we breathe as we stand and stare
at the stars rising one by one,
each its own fire-breathing sun,
at the heavens hovering over our heads
at the flares of fire long after they've fled.

The Land of All Souls

November 2

They are here with us at the breakfast table
sitting in our chairs, buttering their toast,
the knives heavy in their airy hands.
They'd like to eat but are not able.
Food is for the living, not for ghosts.
They drift past us to the window seat.
They survey the day as if making plans.
Who to haunt next, what places they'll go,
how far they can walk on their substanceless feet.
In the end they do what they always do,
stay here with us. They know they are loved,
seen and acknowledged by their flesh & blood.
They move through the day with us, side by side.
They almost believe they're alive.

Awaiting Grace

Advent 2020

It's the season of waiting and we're waiting
for much. A new president, a new grand-
child, a vaccine to save us from ourselves,
the large and the local become as one,
all of it bodied in this small son.
In the dark time of a long dark year
wherein nothing has gone as we had planned,
we are sick of sorrow, fatigued by fear,
hope the horsepower that propels
us forward. Tired of dying, tired of hating,
let's try loving our neighbor for a change,
try finding beauty in the rich and strange
shadows the bare trees cast on the ground,
pray we who are lost can finally be found.

St. Lucy's Fire

December 13th

Dark winter morning for the Feast of Light.
St. Lucy standing at the back door,
a wheel of fire upon her head, each flame
flickering in the shriving wind. Her
face the face of hope, unscored
by time or mortal fret, her left hand
extended as if to ignite the day,
remind us what we came here for, to burn.
What can you teach me, what can I learn
from your shining self? My own name
strange to me even as you speak it.
I am not a saint like you. And yet you stay.
A visitation I had not planned.
Your whole head on fire, my little flame fanned.

The Land of Darkness

Winter Solstice

These the high holy days for worshipers
of darkness. Ice shines in the trees and fires
their inner light. Weather can't kill them now.
They sleep the sleep of the good knowing somehow
the sun that dies today is born tomorrow,
that time is a wheel, not an arrow
that turns in increments as measured as
the heart's. The earth beats to her own slow tune.
The trees bend and pray in the wind. We pass
through on our dusty way while they stay,
patiently waiting for the light to resume
its lease on long delayed summer days.
The god of darkness is a feckless thief.
What he steals from us he cannot keep.

Waiting for Snow

The air is heavy with it, white water
that will tumble from the sky, ragged swatches
of cloud, crystals from the broken ceiling
of the world, all predestined to collude,
collect, and cover over the gray streets,
the pale grass, the sleeping leafless trees,
healing the wounds of winter, revealing
the shape of things lost to too little looking
and less seeing, our eyes weak from lack
of color and light. Welcome interlude
of magic, innocence bodied and brought back
to us after so much darkness and loss.
Bring us our childhood. The world newly birthed.
Proof that nothing is holier than earth.

The Land of Small Mercies

It's winter, time to be kind to the body,
to walk the woods, no matter how windy
and return flushed and full of bright air,
to not fret about how or when or where
your next meal will come, so full is the house
with meat and drink, to not begrudge the mouse
who has built her nest in your house her crumb
from the feast. To sip mulled wine and hot rum,
to warm your hands before the roaring hearth,
to rub shea butter into your cracked heels,
to gaze out the window, observe the dearth
that will be banished by the spring. To feel
amazement at all that you've been given,
to forgive and know that you're forgiven.

The Land of Forgetting

First I lost *anchovy*. Then I lost *cake*.
It was a brain blip. It was a mistake
easily corrected the next day.
Though, honestly, the words arrived too late.
Where it was they went to, I couldn't say.
They slipped out of the fissures in my mind,
wandered off and found another place
to dwell. Even the place I couldn't find,
let alone the words. It is their secret
spot, hidden far away. On my bleakest
days, I doubt they will ever come back.
And then they do, like old friends, guilt wracked
for having left me in my time of need.
I can't stanch the wound. Word by word I bleed.

The Land of Seeing

Here comes morning with all of her charm,
all of her daily beauty. Here comes
rain, soft and small, falling on the firm
earth. Here come thirsty worms. Here come
hungry birds. And here the soft-pawed cat.
Every day the world returns outside
my door. Every day I watch, hope to catch
some small revelation trying to hide
its magic self from me. I want to see
like a blind woman who's just retrieved
her sight, like a sleeper who wakes relieved
to have survived the night and knows she's
just received a gift she can't return,
like a fool who has everything to learn.

In The Land of Perfection

moves the small miracle of the chipmunk
who noses his way along the cracks
separating the stones that make up the back
patio, who inches his perfect humped-up
body along, probing the dirt with his
perfect nose, finding something that is
invisible & delectable to his chipmunk
tongue, oblivious to the brickwork,
the wrought-iron gate, the cypresses ten feet tall,
the serpentine wall enclosing us all
in its sturdy embrace, to the white sky
that hovers, dropping morning rain on my
basil, tomatoes, the wild rose that grows
in the corner, the chipmunk, his perfect nose.

The Land of Desire

You have made us for yourself, O Lord,
and our hearts are restless until they rest in you.
                    —St. Augustine

I want, I want, I want, my heart sings.
Names and places, continents, lovely things
to soothe the throb and shut her bleeding trap.
All she does is complain, complain, complain.
As if crying will get her what she wants.
She knows that is just a load of crap.
Desire is endless. It makes us insane.
It is the twin that's born with us and haunts
our racing days. It never goes away
until we do. It's the one thing that stays
constant in the midst of every change.
Think of it, heart. Imagine how strange
silence will be when you no longer beat,
you who sing *I want* even as we sleep.

V

Literary Islands

"Much have I traveled in the realms of gold."

—JOHN KEATS, "On First Looking into Chapman's Homer"

Conjure

"Art is our chief means of breaking bread with the dead."
—*W. H. Auden*

And break it they do with the likes of me
and you, tear it off in great ragged pieces,
stuff it in their gobs, wash it down with tea
(milk white, two sugars). How it eases
them, eating again, satisfies their hunger
for food and for talk, soothes their anger
at the outrage of having to be dead.
They never knew how much they would miss bread
until it was denied them. And here we
come, armed with stone and paint and poems,
to woo them back to life with pen or palette knife,
gifts we give them they can never own,
when what they really want is bread, sweet tea,
to be alive again with you and me.

Listen! He Said, So I Did

St. John's Abbey
Collegeville, Minnesota

Listen! he said, so I did.
Listen with the ear of your heart.

Heart which has the word *hear* in it.
And I hearted the loon on the lake.

I hearted the skyful of blue.
I hearted the grass, for pity's sake,

it made so much noise growing.
I hearted the sunlit leaves on the trees.

I hearted the old monk rowing
his boat across Lake Sagatagan.

The stones preach to me about Jesus
as I make my morning run,

my heart hearting hard as a racehorse
galloping up the Abbey Road

while I heart George Harrison's
My Sweet Lord (there's no escaping Jesus)

and heart McCartney's naked feet
padding across the pavement.

There is so much to heart
and so little time

I've started to heart in my sleep.
The air conditioner,

the plastic blinds that keep
time to the bathroom fan.

The voice of a monastic man
holding a book, pen in his hand

inscribing a word on the blank
page of the past,

calling to me across the vast
range of space and of years

balm to these aching ears,
now writ on my hearing heart

the word,
both first and last.

Listen! he says,
with the ear of your art.

Visitations

Stumpf Lake
Collegeville, Minnesota

I'm sitting here on my brick back porch
watching the saints walk by. Funny how they
know where to find me, no matter how far away
I go from the comforts of home. I leave
the doors unlocked, light up the Tiki torch,
send smoke signals only they can read:
Here waits a poet in desperate need
of a roadmap of her own mind,
who misses the friends she left behind
who keep her honest and make her good.
And sure enough, here they come. Melville,
Flannery, Sinatra, my Mom. They would
stop and stay if they could, sit down a spell,
tell me the next story I have to tell.

Melville's Soliloquy

August 1, 2019
Melville's 200th Birthday
Collegeville, Minnesota

"Talk not to me of blasphemy, man.
I'd strike the sun if it insulted me."
—Moby Dick, or The Whale

The lake knows nothing of my madness.
It slides and glides in the northern sun
ignorant of the fish that breathe beneath
its coddled waters. Their calm can't ease
my wild mind. All my years of restless
pursuit of the uncatchable have come
to this—
          an old man standing on the shore
of dribbling streams in a landlocked state
as far from the sea as it's possible to be.
I once dreamed of creatures bigger than their God.
No matter how grand, no matter how odd
my books were, they could not satiate
the ravening hunger that I was born for.
The absence of wind shakes me to the core.

Flannery's Last Day

August 3
Anniversary of Flannery O'Connor's Death

Today of all days you would show up
making sure you are not forgotten.
Your suffering at the end was true,
fever, nausea, coma, and all you
wanted was another day of life
even if you spent it throwing up.
Your bed was sweaty, the sheets sodden
with Georgia summer, the air rife
with peaches growing outside the door.
And still you wanted more.
In your final dreams you were thinking up
new stories that needed to be told,
bonkers plots that would never unfold,
a sick woman who rises up and grows old.

The Land of Andalusia

"Pilgrims to Flannery O'Connor's home frequently gather dirt from beneath the front porch and seal it in small bottles."
—Literary Devotions

For ten years it sat on my window sill,
the vial of clay from Flannery's farm,
a gift from a friend who had visited
that hallowed spot, made a pilgrimage
to the shrine of our secular saint.
I thought it was charming, thought it was quaint
that he would assume I wanted it.
The dust gathered dust. It did no harm,
but no good either. It did not fill
a need I had. The gift gratuitous
like most things that are sweet and useless.
I loved the giver more than the gift
until the day I threw it away.
I miss it now more than I can say.

The Feast of St. Seamus

August 20th

"I rhyme to see myself, to set the darkness echoing."
—*Seamus Heaney*

For years I've knelt at your holy wells
and envied the cut of your clean-edged song,
lay down in the bog where dead men dwell,
grieved with your ghosts who told of their wrongs.
Your consonants cleave my soft palate.
I taste their rough music and savor it long
past the last line of the taut sonnet,
its rhyming subtle, its accent strong.
And every poem speaks a sacrament,
blood of old blessing and bread of the word,
feeding me full in language as ancient
as Aran's rock and St. Kevin's birds.
English will never be the same.
To make it ours is why you came.

Glasnevin Graveyard

"Mine, O thou lord of life, send my roots rain."
—*Gerard Manley Hopkins*

Walking these grounds
I nearly hear you
in the finch-feather-fall,
the summer-clover-clamor.

Under rain gray sky,
a soft day, the Irish would say,
you lie in strange earth
poet among the dead and dumb.

I wander cinder paths
and find you far
from the splendor of Parnell's rock,
neat crosses of decent Dubliners.

Yet you are not alone,
a name engraved on a single stone
inscribed with scores of others,
a mass of priestly brothers.

A few Latin syllables
claim your space for eternity.
Beneath these grieving yews
you've taken root.

Withered now to ash
beyond this brief burning
refined past reckoning
even your bones sing.

The Days When Only Rilke Will Do

"I can imagine no knowledge more blessed than this:
that one must become a beginner . . .
come back to the place of naiveté."
—Rainer Maria Rilke

The days when only Rilke will do
arrive and I know nothing is truer
than these wounds, this blue-bled sky,
the white birch weeping from its yellow eye.
The childless birds, their summer blather
past, now nest down, forage and gather
leavings of our season of excess.
They do not mind the bitterness
of berries too long left upon the vine.
No red regret darkens the birdish mind.

Come. Let's walk into the fields
past the river and its purling song,
sink our sins, gray stones, into the pond,
remember how innocence feels.

The Land of Lickwidge

I dreamt a strange new lickwidge last night.
Flugeforth, I said, *Dear Danderling.*
They eyed me skisically, begbite
I blouted it just the same. I flang
words like they was prunebics, soft & ush.
They frattered on the kood gloor like flums.
Where did they come from, these geezy blix?
And where did my slook benes get to?
I was plumfluffle in a flintflot
wrecking the welf, setting all the shix
on flame. I was glip, I was rampin red hot.
But none of it phlent nothin' to you.
I glabbed you by the glumpus. I blist your flup.
You said *Dear Danderling* & I woke up.

Postcard from Purgatory #1

"And I will sing of that second realm where the human spirit purges itself and becomes worthy to ascend to heaven." —Purgatorio, I, 3–6

Dear Mom,
        It's fine here, I'm surprised to say.
Much better than I thought it would be.
My room is clean, though the hotel is seedy.
The roaches are small and sleep during the day.
The pool is full of algae and slime,
a thick stew of *goo chartreuse*. Yet I find
swimming in it cures my blues. There's no time
to wallow in guilt and rue. They keep
us busy. Gentle devils cheer as we
fail and try, time & time again, to climb
steep hills of garbage, compost of our sin.
We get to the top and slide down again.
When we run on hot coals, I come in first.
It's no spring picnic, but I've seen worse.

VI

Border Songs

"Something there is that doesn't love a wall."

—ROBERT FROST, "Mending Wall"

Border Songs
A Mercy of Triolets

United States–Mexico Border
Spring 2019

Border Song #1

Say, stolen child, the world from which you've come.
You can't go back, although you know you must.
Your father grieves, your mother is undone.
Say, stolen child, the world from which you've come.
You, their only daughter. You, their only son.
All their dreams are now turned to dust.
Say, stolen child, the world from which you've come.
You can't go back, although you know you must.

Border Song #2

They confiscate your rosary when you come.
I cannot go to sleep without one.
Thumbing each bead until the night is done.
They confiscate your rosary when you come.
There's nowhere to hide it. Nowhere to run.
It was my dead mother's. Now I have none.
They confiscate your rosary when you come.
I cannot go to sleep without one.

Border Song #3

I came with just a hairbrush and a watch
to keep my beauty and to keep track of time.
They took them both the morning I was caught.
I came with just a hairbrush and a watch.
Food was what I craved. Work was what I sought.
Now none of these fine things can be made mine.
I came with just a hairbrush and a watch.
I've lost my beauty and lost all track of time.

Border Song #4

My child sleeps in a cage and yet he sings
like the birds of paradise we left behind.
Knowing nothing of the fear the future brings
my child sleeps in a cage and yet he sings.
The children in the States live like kings.
The lies they told us haunt my waking mind.
My child sleeps in a cage and yet he sings
like the birds of paradise we left behind.

Border Song #5

I dream of corn tortillas and black beans
and eat the food the white men bring to me.
White bread and bologna. Canned green beans.
I dream of corn tortillas and black beans.
Old and poor, a man of little means,
I took my buen provecho beneath the banyan tree.
I dream of those tortillas and black beans
and eat the food the white men bring to me.

Border Song #6

Seventy-six women locked inside a cell
made for twelve. This is a little hell.
We cannot bathe. We cannot stand our smell.
Seventy-six women locked inside a cell.
Some of us are sick. None of us is well.
Seventy-six women dying in a cell
made for twelve. Welcome to our hell.

Border Song #7

I lost my country. Now I've lost my mind.
I did not know the price would be so high,
that they would hate me since I'm not their kind.
I lost my country. Now I've lost my mind,
despise the skin I'm bound in. I have consigned
myself to exile in a place where I will die.
I lost my country. Now I've lost my mind.
I did not know the price would be so high.

Border Song #8

Sing me freedom. Sing me some good news.
Sing a song it heals my heart to hear.
I'm all alone. My only friend's the blues.
Sing me freedom. Sing me some good news.
They stole my shoestrings and they stole my shoes.
But shod or not, I'm walking out of here.
Sing me freedom. Sing me your good news.
Sing a song it heals my heart to hear.

Border Song #9

I am a father, though I have no son.
They wrested him away and now he's gone.
I had no knife, no passport, no gun.
I am a father, though I have no son.
They took away my moon. They took my sun.
All I do is weep from dusk to dawn.
I am a father, though I have no son.
They wrested him away and now he's gone.

Border Song #10

Nothing is bluer than the Texas sky.
I watch it through the spaces in the bars.
Birds fly through it and clouds drift by.
Nothing is bluer than the Texas sky.
It lifts my heart. I don't know why.
At night it goes black. Then I see the stars.
Nothing is bluer than the Texas sky.
I watch it through the spaces in the bars.

Border Song #11

I don't know what it means to be alone.
I live with other strangers night and day.
I have no time or space to call my own.
I don't know what it means to be alone.
I never would have come if I had known
I would be forced to give my soul away.
I don't know what it means to be alone.
I live with other strangers night and day.

Border Song #12

We kill the children at the border.
This is the way we set them free.
It's not our fault. We follow orders.
We kill the children at the border.
A hard life is better if it's shorter.
Things aren't the way they imagine them to be.
We kill the children at the border.
This is the way we set them free.

Border Song #13

Our country has a border crisis.
Our president eats cake and tweets.
It's much less fun than fighting ISIS.
Our country has a border crisis.
A rich man doesn't know how priceless
freedom is. He eats and eats.
Our country has a border crisis.
Our president eats cake and tweets.

Border Song #14

I woke to rain gentle on my skin
falling from the sky into my holding pen.
It wet my lips and dribbled down my chin.
I woke to rain gentle on my skin.
It tasted like home, the sweetest place I've been.
I dreamt I was back in my country again.
I woke to rain gentle on my skin
falling from the sky into my holding pen.

Border Song #15

Face down in the river lies a father.
Beside him lies his little daughter.
The saddest death is death by water.
He held her when the current caught her.
He did not leave. He did not falter.
Face down in the river lies a father.
His arms around his little daughter.

One Story

There are only two stories: a person goes
on a journey or a stranger comes to town.
We venture out from our own small house,
we find a new place and we settle down
until the story starts again. We know
the two are truly one. We leave and we come.
To loathe one country is to love the next.
This double life will never be done
until we're out of breath, until brother death
escorts us on one final trip to where
we cannot say. The flight plan isn't shared.
We travel east while we are heading west.
On this one fact every tale depends:
we start the story to get to the end.

AFTERWORD

This book began in The Holy Land.

Two years ago, I embarked on a 12-day pilgrimage, one of a group of 12 travelers. Given these apostolic numbers, from the get-go, everything about this trip loomed biblical. After our long journey from New York to Tel Aviv, we drove to Galilee and spent our first night at the Mount of the Beatitudes, where, tradition has it, Christ delivered those deathless words of blessing to the crowds that gathered there.

I woke early the next day and went out for my morning run, a ritual I've been practicing for 40 years—another biblical number—only this particular morning I found myself running along the Sea of Galilee, a place I had seen often in my mind's eye, but never with my body's.

As I ran and watched the sun rise over the water, I felt the spell of this holy place. Looking out over the calm lake, I saw a man in a small boat caught in a storm, along with his fellow fishermen. He stood up in the boat, which pitched and rolled with every wave, his robes blowing wildly in the wind, raised his arms, and as suddenly as the storm had come, he stilled it.

By the time I returned to my room, I had composed in my mind the opening lines of "The Storm Chaser," the poem that generated this book.

This was the first of a series of Christ Sightings I experienced while traveling through Palestine and Israel. As I followed in the footsteps of Jesus, from Bethlehem to Nazareth, Magdala to Jericho, the River Jordan to the Dead Sea, the Mount of Olives to Calvary, Christ seemed to be following me. While my traveling companions took photographs of these storied places, I tried to capture them—and my glimpses of him—in poems.

After I left the Holy Land, this accompaniment did not stop. Jesus continued to show up—in New York, Baltimore, Minnesota, North Carolina, Arizona, and Florida—among other places I visited. I gradually came to acknowledge the fact that these Christ Sightings have been a constant, a phenomenon happening my whole life. Christ does not confine himself to the place christened "The Holy Land"—he is a world traveler. The tally of his frequent flyer miles would astonish.

When I was child, growing up Catholic, our religious instruction consisted mostly of memorizing the Baltimore Catechism. One of the questions the Catechism poses is "Where is God?" The answer, of course, is "God is everywhere." We believed this to be true. God was in church, but God was also in our house (a crucifix in every room), in the backyard, in our Buick (rosary beads swinging from the rearview mirror), at our birthday parties in the basement, and in our own bodies. And though those places may not sound very holy, they were. Because God was there. Is there.

The poems in this book affirm this foundational belief—that all places are holy places, all land is Holy Land. In addition, they extend the terrain, moving beyond the geographical and the physical to the temporal, the carnal, the intellectual, and the spiritual realms. Our days are blessed, our bodies are blessed, our minds and spirits are blessed terrain.

The poet Gerard Manley Hopkins once wrote, "The world is charged with the grandeur of God." This is not to say that the world—holy as it is—is not also a troubled and troubling place. In another poem, the same poet also prays, "I wake and feel the fell of dark, not day." Even in a state of desolation, the poet knew the night is no less holy than the day. The body no less holy than the soul. The experience of death no less holy than life. Creation is all of a piece.

The English word *holy* is related to the Germanic word *heilig*, a word that means *blessed* and also carries within it the idea of *wholeness*. These poems attempt to honor the holiness and the wholeness of our world—from Gotham to Golgotha, the Bronx River to the Sea of Galilee—and to honor the holiness and wholeness of our blessed and broken humanity.

ANGELA ALAIMO O'DONNELL
October 31, 2021
Bronx, New York

ACKNOWLEDGMENTS

I am grateful to the editors of the following publications in which some of the poems in this book first appeared, some under different titles or in slightly different versions:

A Given Grace: An Anthology of Christian Poems: "Christ Sighting: Advent," "Christ Sighting: The Land of Resurrection," "St. Lucy's Fire," "Son God"

Alabama Literary Review, "Postcard from Purgatory #1"

America: "The Feast of St. Seamus," "Lazarus"

Bearings Online: "The Early Birds," "*Listen!* He Said, So I Did"

Christian Century: "Easter Monday," "Magdalene's Mistake," "The Women"

Evangelization & Culture: "The Storm Chaser," "The Thief," "Via Dolorosa," "*Ichthys* at the Jordan," "The Mount of Olives," "The Church of the Nativity"

Italian Americana: "Consecration"

Keystone Poets Anthology: "Immigrant Song"

Measure: "Tell Me"

Poets Reading the News: "Borderlands: A Mercy of Triolets"

Post Road: "Tigh Mholly"

Presence: A Journal of Catholic Poetry: "Conjure"

Vineyards: "Carrowmore"

Windhover: "Glasnevin Graveyard," "Hopkins in Ireland"

I am grateful to the good people of Paraclete Press, especially editor Jon Sweeney, who have done me the honor of awarding me the Paraclete Poetry Prize 2021 for *Holy Land*. Thank you to judges Laura Reece Hogan and Scott Cairns, whose work I have so long admired, for your faith in this book.

I am also grateful to the many friends, family members, colleagues, and fellow writers who have offered encouragement in connection with these poems and this project. Among these are my colleagues at Fordham University, especially Maria Terzulli & Christine Firer Hinze, and the many friends who are part of the virtual poetry community I am blessed to belong to. I am grateful to my friends at the Collegeville Institute at St. John's University in Minnesota, where I was fortunate to have spent ten days in a writer's residency as part of the *A Part Yet Apart* program and where a number of these poems were written. In addition, I am grateful to my fellow pilgrims to the Holy Land and to the students of Bethlehem University in Palestine, who served as the first audience for the poem that generated this book, "The Storm Chaser." Their enthusiastic response convinced me that this project was worth pursuing.

Last but never least, I am grateful, as ever, to my family, who have embraced my poetry these many years and who inspire me every day by their example of how to live a loving, richly creative, holy life. I am especially grateful to my husband, Brennan, for our long and joyful pursuit of the literary life together and who has served generously and faithfully as my first and best reader.

O that my words were written down!
O that they were inscribed in a book!
O that with an iron pen and with lead
they were engraved on a rock forever!
—JOB 19:23–24

IRON PEN

Outcast and utterly alone, Job pours out his anguish to his Maker. From the depths of his pain, he reveals a trust in God's goodness that is stronger than his despair, giving humanity some of the most beautiful and poetic verses of all time. Paraclete's Iron Pen imprint is inspired by this spirit of unvarnished honesty and tenacious hope.

ABOUT PARACLETE PRESS

Paraclete Press is the publishing arm of the Cape Cod Benedictine community, the Community of Jesus. Presenting a full expression of Christian belief and practice, we reflect the ecumenical charism of the Community and its dedication to sacred music, the fine arts, and the written word.

SCAN
TO
READ
MORE

www.paracletepress.com

YOU MAY ALSO ENJOY THESE COLLECTIONS BY ANGELA ALAIMO O'DONNELL . . .

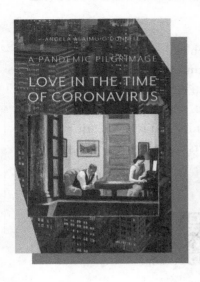

www.paracletepress.com